A SNAPSHOT™ BOOK

SNAPSHOT™ is an imprint of Covent Garden Books.
95 Madison Avenue
New York, NY 10016

Every effort has been made to
trace the copyright holders and we
apologize in advance for any unintentional
omissions. We would be pleased to insert
the appropriate acknowledgment in any
subsequent edition of this publication.

ISBN 1-56458-727-4

Color reproduction by Colourscan
Printed and bound in Belgium by Proost

SNAP SHOT™

Senior Editor
Mary Ling

Editor
Finbar Hawkins

Art Editor
Joanna Pocock

Designer
Jane Bull

Production
Catherine Semark

Consultant
Sue Copsey

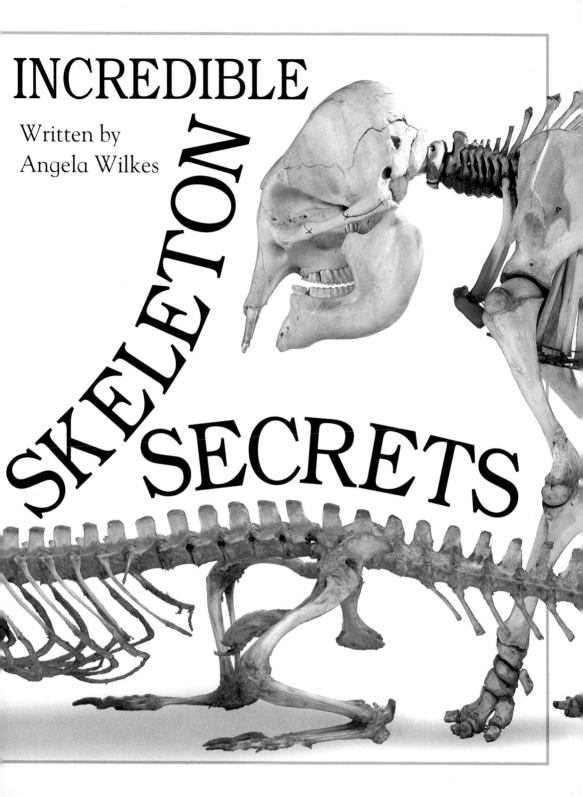

INCREDIBLE

Written by
Angela Wilkes

SKELETON SECRETS

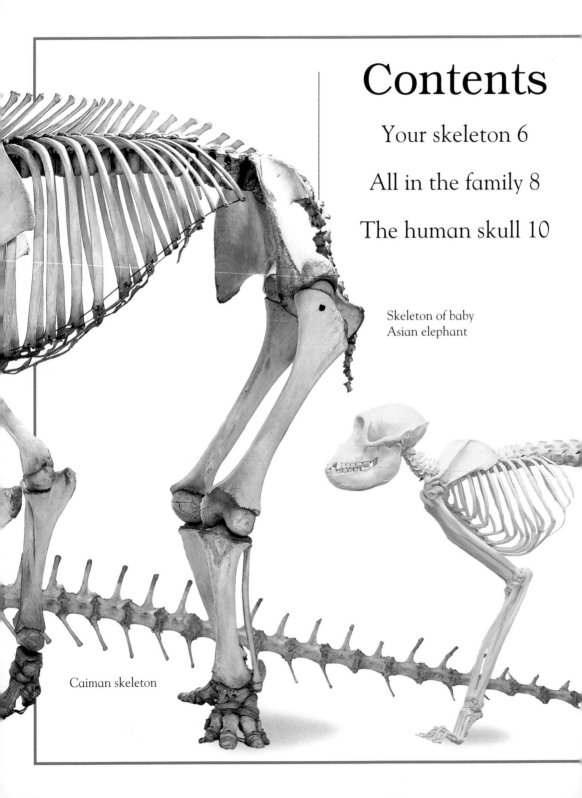

Contents

Skeleton of baby
Asian elephant

Caiman skeleton

Rhesus
monkey
skeleton

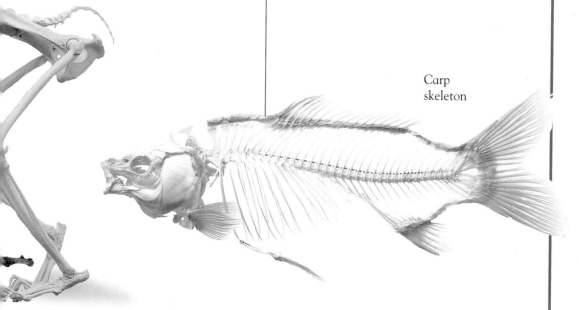

Carp
skeleton

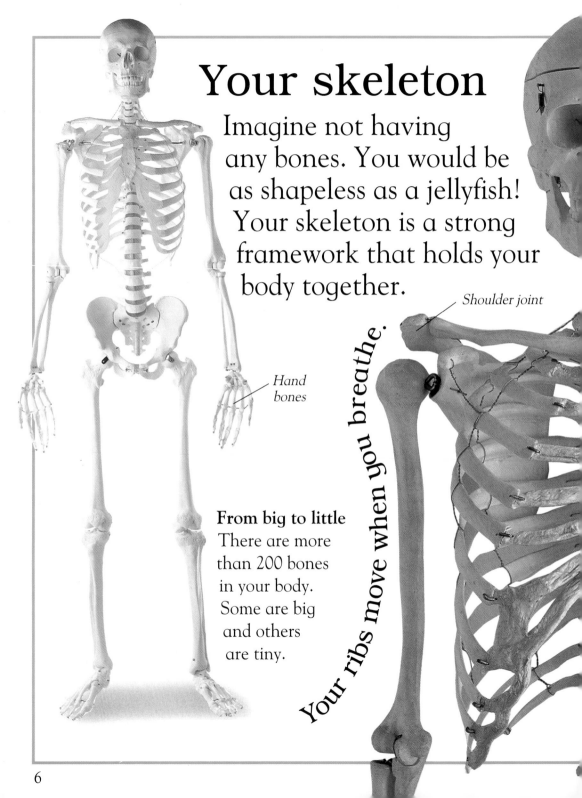

Your skeleton

Imagine not having any bones. You would be as shapeless as a jellyfish! Your skeleton is a strong framework that holds your body together.

Shoulder joint

Hand bones

Your ribs move when you breathe.

From big to little
There are more than 200 bones in your body. Some are big and others are tiny.

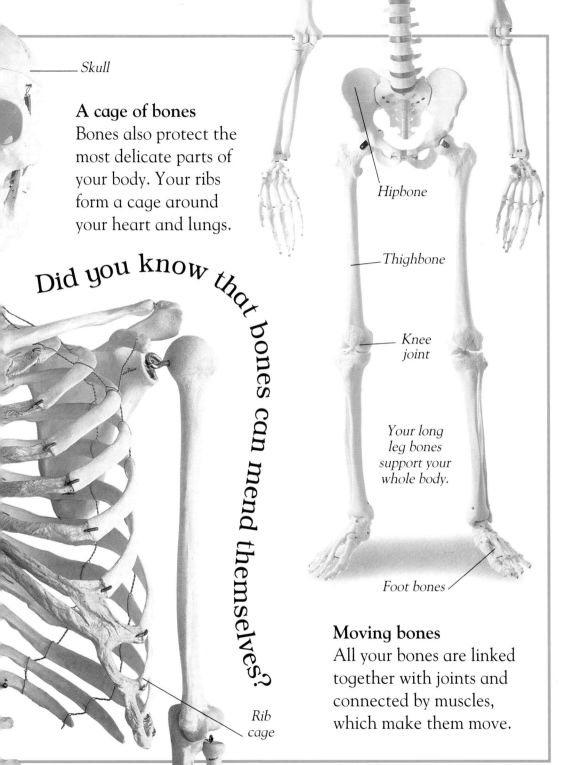

Skull

A cage of bones
Bones also protect the most delicate parts of your body. Your ribs form a cage around your heart and lungs.

Hipbone

Did you know that bones can mend themselves?

Thighbone

Knee joint

Your long leg bones support your whole body.

Foot bones

Rib cage

Moving bones
All your bones are linked together with joints and connected by muscles, which make them move.

All in the family

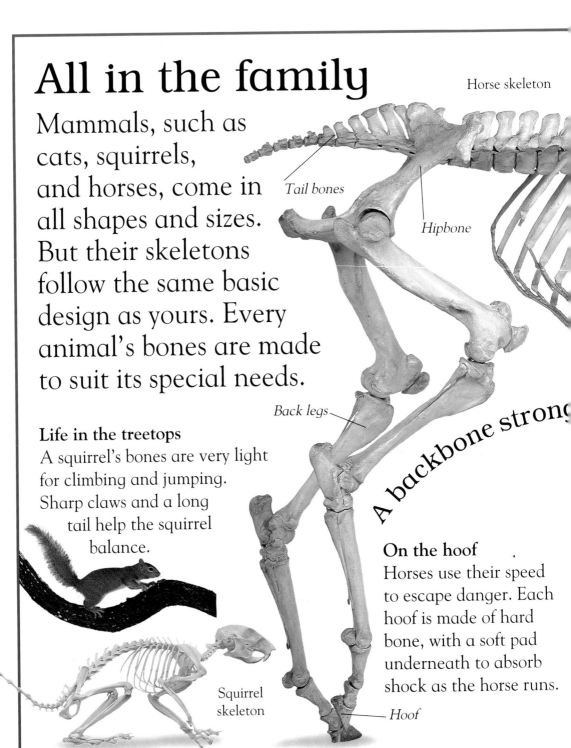

Horse skeleton

Mammals, such as cats, squirrels, and horses, come in all shapes and sizes. But their skeletons follow the same basic design as yours. Every animal's bones are made to suit its special needs.

Tail bones

Hipbone

Back legs

A backbone strong

Life in the treetops
A squirrel's bones are very light for climbing and jumping. Sharp claws and a long tail help the squirrel balance.

On the hoof
Horses use their speed to escape danger. Each hoof is made of hard bone, with a soft pad underneath to absorb shock as the horse runs.

Squirrel skeleton

Hoof

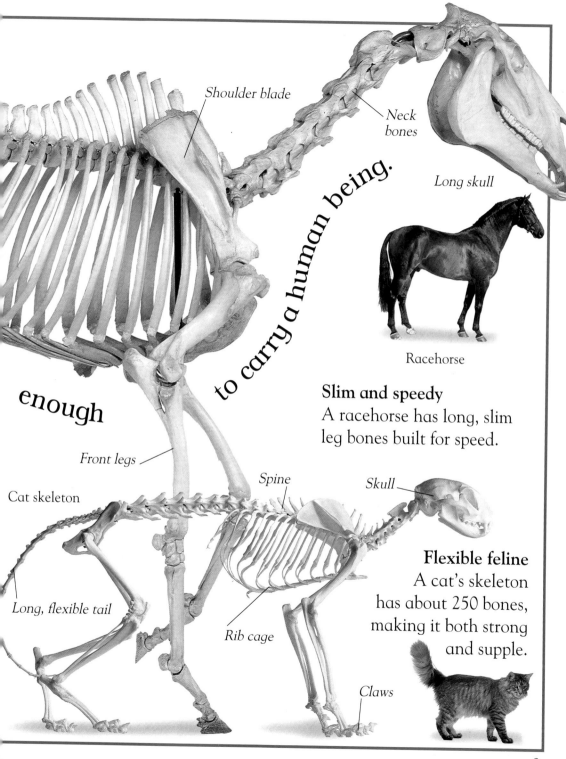

Shoulder blade

Neck bones

Long skull

to carry a human being.

enough

Racehorse

Slim and speedy
A racehorse has long, slim leg bones built for speed.

Front legs

Cat skeleton

Spine

Skull

Flexible feline
A cat's skeleton has about 250 bones, making it both strong and supple.

Long, flexible tail

Rib cage

Claws

9

The human skull

Your skull is a safe box for your most important organ – the brain! Without your brain you couldn't eat, breathe, digest, or dream.

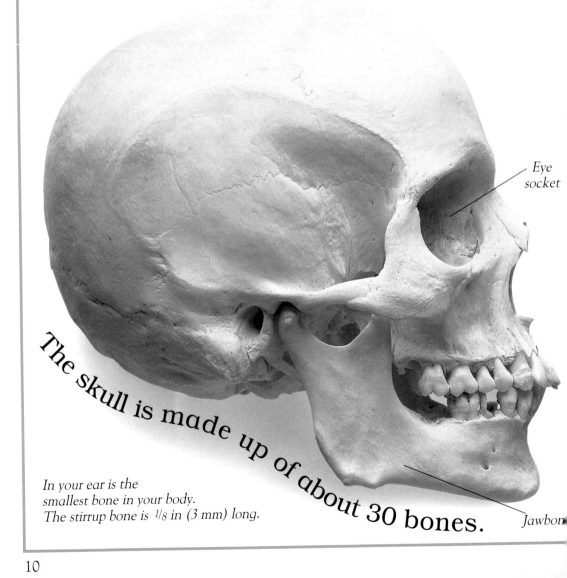

Eye socket

In your ear is the smallest bone in your body. The stirrup bone is ⅛ in (3 mm) long.

The skull is made up of about 30 bones.

Jawbone

Control center for the body

Skull bones also protect your eyes and ears. In fact, your senses of sight, hearing, taste, and smell are all controlled from your brain.

A child has 20 teeth and an adult has 32.

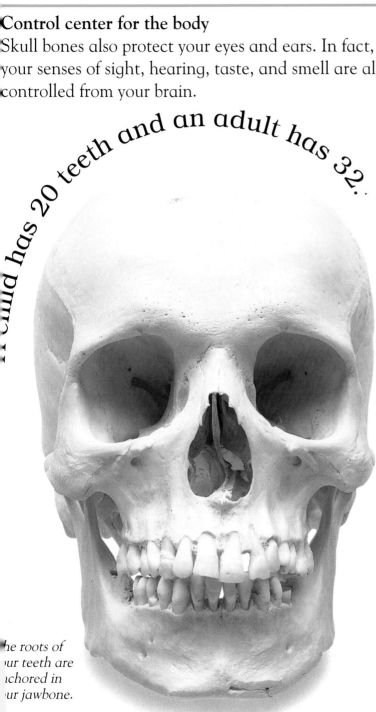

The roots of your teeth are anchored in your jawbone.

Muscle power
There are more than 100 muscles in your face.

Making faces
You use about 30 of your face muscles every minute to show what you are feeling.

Head cases

Some animal skulls are long and skinny, others short and stout. Som[e] have horns and some have a snout. Each skull is specially adapted to an animal's way of life.

Good vision is essential for life in the trees.

A parrot's huge, hooked beak is useful for cracking nuts.

A lion's well-muscled jaw

Lion skull

Needle-sharp teeth for grasping fish

Gharial skull

Killer jaws

A lion's massive jaws and huge fangs are built-in weapons for killing prey.

means a powerful bite.

Identifying feature

An antelope's corkscrew horns grow from the top of its skull. Sometimes they stretch to about 4 ft (1.5 m) long!

Twisted horns are made of bone with a horny casing.

A firm grip

A lion's canine teeth are rooted deep in the skull to strengthen its hold on prey.

Sneaky snout!

A sly gharial lurks low in the water. Its eyes and nose are on top of its skull so it can breathe and see above the water.

nostrils

Antelope skull

13

Terrible teeth

Is it a nibbler, crusher, or grinder?
You can tell a lot about an animal
and the kind of food it eats from
the shape of its teeth.

Jaws you never want to meet!

The heaviest tooth in the world!

Elephant
tusk

Jaws!
A shark's teeth
only last about 10
days, so new ones
grow to replace
the teeth
in front.

Long in the tooth
Elephants' ivory tusks
are teeth which never
stop growing. They are
useful as tools and as weapons.

Lower jaw

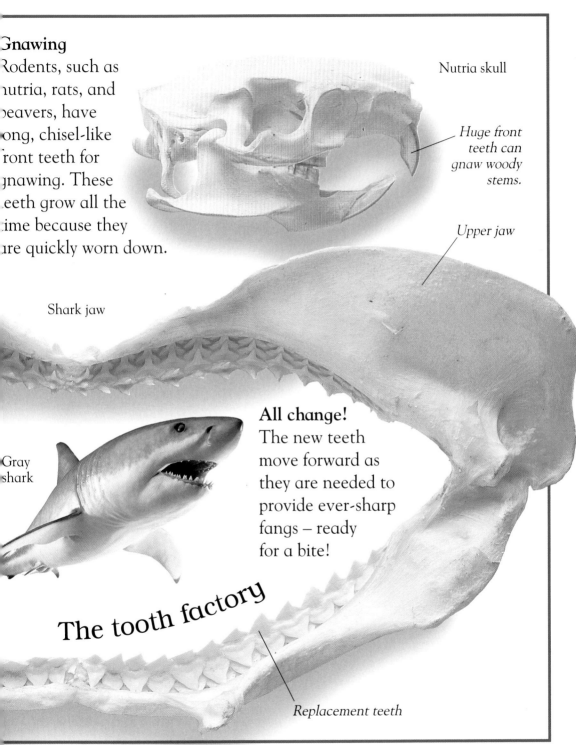

Gnawing

Rodents, such as nutria, rats, and beavers, have long, chisel-like front teeth for gnawing. These teeth grow all the time because they are quickly worn down.

Nutria skull

Huge front teeth can gnaw woody stems.

Upper jaw

Shark jaw

All change!

The new teeth move forward as they are needed to provide ever-sharp fangs – ready for a bite!

Gray shark

The tooth factory

Replacement teeth

Plenty of backbone

Your spine is like a rod for your head, arms, and legs. It is made of 24 small bones, called vertebrae, linked together. This is why you can bend and twist your body.

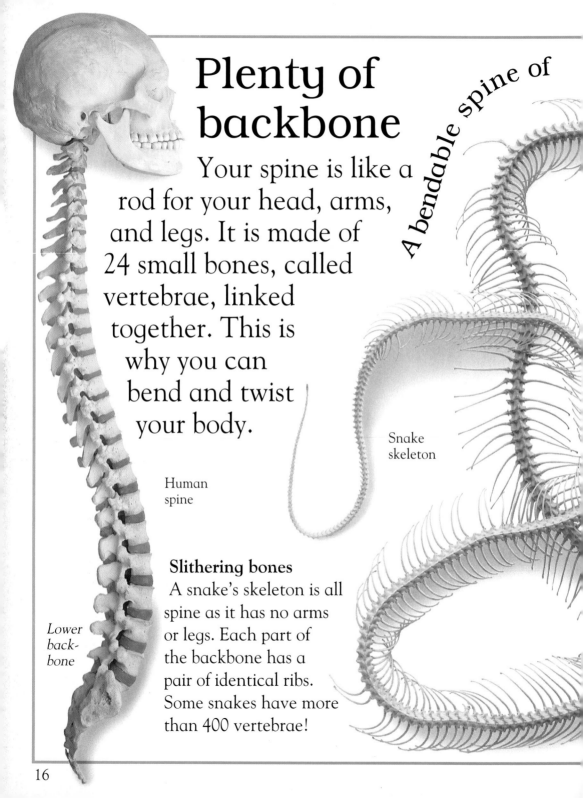

Snake skeleton

Human spine

Lower back-bone

Slithering bones
A snake's skeleton is all spine as it has no arms or legs. Each part of the backbone has a pair of identical ribs. Some snakes have more than 400 vertebrae!

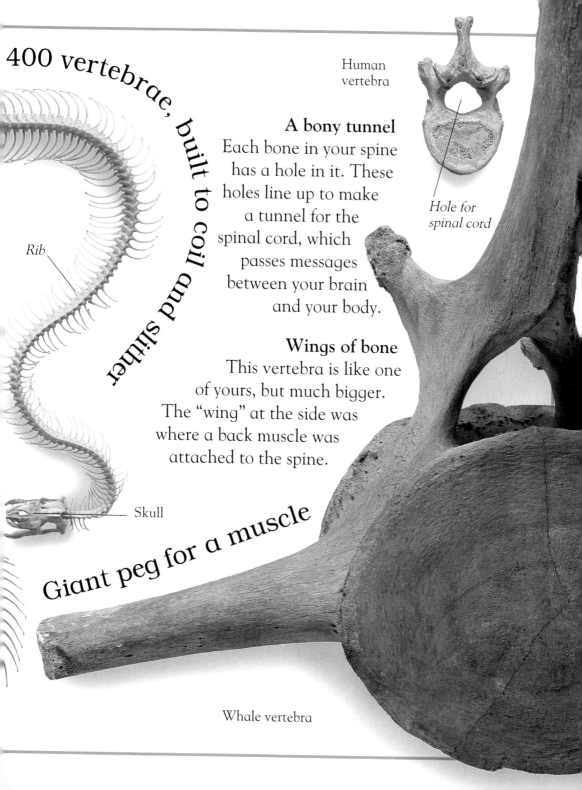

400 vertebrae, built to coil and slither

Rib

Skull

Human vertebra

A bony tunnel
Each bone in your spine has a hole in it. These holes line up to make a tunnel for the spinal cord, which passes messages between your brain and your body.

Hole for spinal cord

Wings of bone
This vertebra is like one of yours, but much bigger. The "wing" at the side was where a back muscle was attached to the spine.

Giant peg for a muscle

Whale vertebra

From shoulder to fingertip

Your arms are really a series of amazing levers with sensitive pincers at the end. Other animals have adapted their "arms" for different uses.

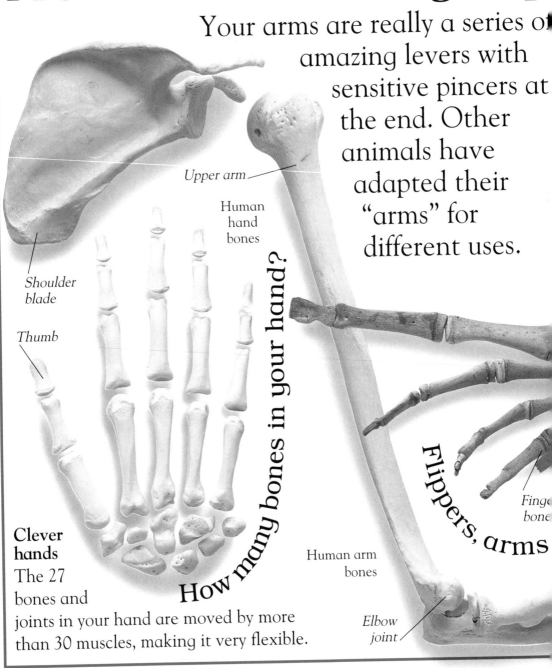

Upper arm

Human hand bones

Shoulder blade

Thumb

How many bones in your hand?

Clever hands

The 27 bones and joints in your hand are moved by more than 30 muscles, making it very flexible.

Human arm bones

Elbow joint

Flippers, arms

Finger bone

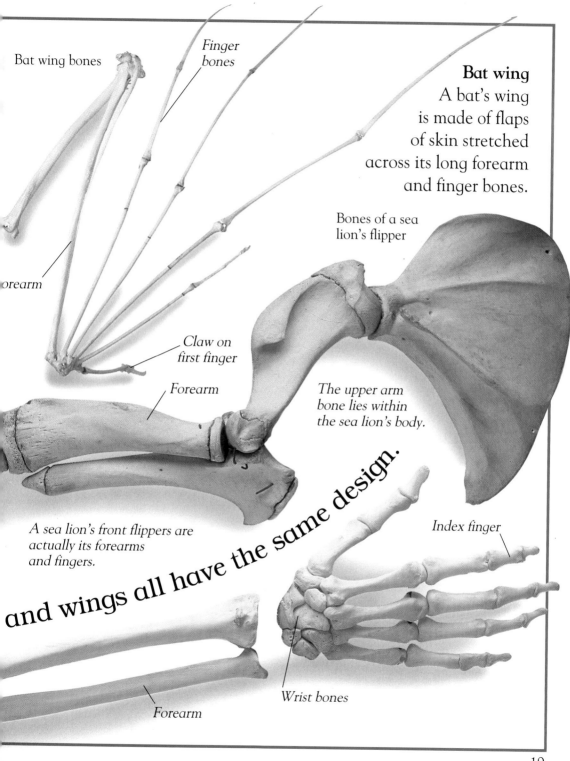

Bat wing bones

Finger bones

Bat wing
A bat's wing is made of flaps of skin stretched across its long forearm and finger bones.

Bones of a sea lion's flipper

orearm

Claw on first finger

Forearm

The upper arm bone lies within the sea lion's body.

A sea lion's front flippers are actually its forearms and fingers.

and wings all have the same design.

Index finger

Wrist bones

Forearm

Thighbone

Looking at legs

Standing and walking on two legs the way we do is an incredible balancing act. Most animals walk on four legs, with their weight on their toes.

A spring in your step ...

Load-bearing pillars

Your leg bones need to be strong to support your weight. Your feet are broad and long to help you balance.

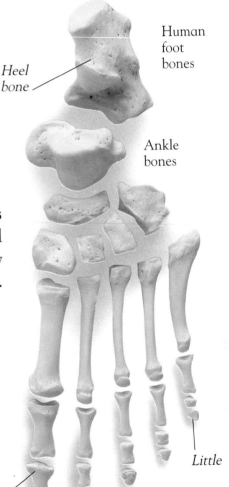

Human foot bones

Heel bone

Ankle bones

Toes like fingers

Your foot is made of 26 small bones. These provide a springy base that makes walking easy.

Fold-away legs

Frog back leg bones

A frog's thigh, calf, and foot are all about the same length. They straighten out when the frog jumps, to give extra spring.

Big toe

Little

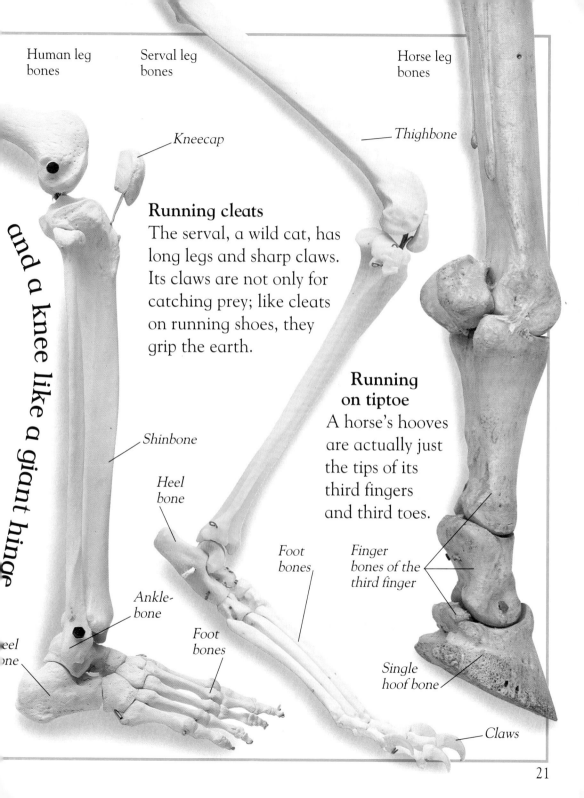

Human leg bones

Serval leg bones

Horse leg bones

Kneecap

Thighbone

Running cleats
The serval, a wild cat, has long legs and sharp claws. Its claws are not only for catching prey; like cleats on running shoes, they grip the earth.

Running on tiptoe
A horse's hooves are actually just the tips of its third fingers and third toes.

Shinbone

Heel bone

Foot bones

Finger bones of the third finger

Ankle-bone

Foot bones

Single hoof bone

eel one

Claws

and a knee like a giant hinge

Flying skeletons

It would be hard to fly with heavy bones like ours. But birds' skeletons are built for flight. Their bones are light and often hollow. Birds also have beaks instead of heavy teeth.

Skull

Long, thin wing bones

Paper-thin skull
Birds have thin skull bones and large eye sockets, to keep their weight low.

Wing bones

Horny beak over jaws

Claws

Skeleton of a bird

Breastbone

Even keel
A bird's breastbone has a special keel or ridge. The keel acts as an anchor for the powerful muscles that make the bird's wings flap.

An airy frame
Some of a bird's hollow bones have air sacs, which increase the bird's lightness and help it breathe more efficiently.

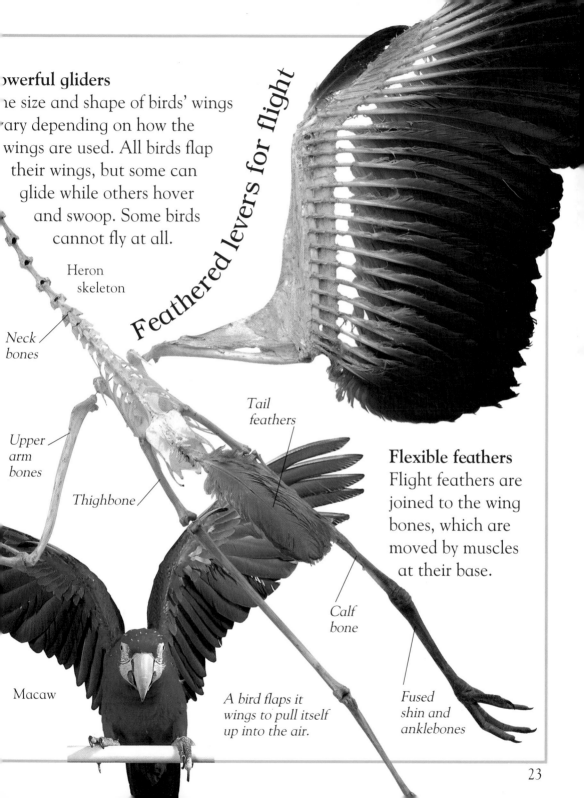

Powerful gliders
The size and shape of birds' wings vary depending on how the wings are used. All birds flap their wings, but some can glide while others hover and swoop. Some birds cannot fly at all.

Heron skeleton

Neck bones

Upper arm bones

Thighbone

Tail feathers

Feathered levers for flight

Flexible feathers
Flight feathers are joined to the wing bones, which are moved by muscles at their base.

Calf bone

Macaw

A bird flaps it wings to pull itself up into the air.

Fused shin and anklebones

Fish bones

Like you, fish have skeletons inside their bodies. In fact, 500 million years ago, they were the first ever animals to have a backbone. But unlike most land animals, fish have no arms or legs.

A streamlined skeleton, built for spee

Skeleton story
This cod skeleton is typical of most bony fish. It has a skull, a backbone, and a "fin skeleton."

Dorsal fin

Ventral fins

Fin skeleton
The fish's fins and tail, which it uses for steering, are anchored firmly in its body by a framework of bones and rods.

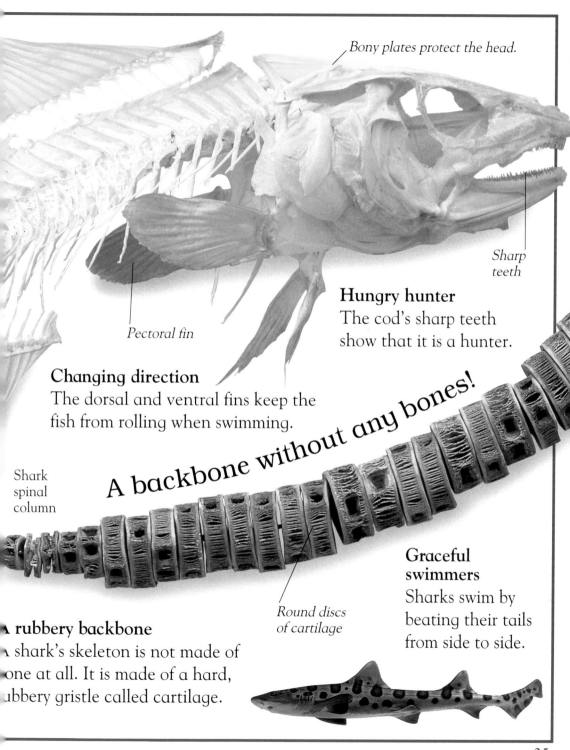

Bony plates protect the head.

Sharp teeth

Pectoral fin

Hungry hunter
The cod's sharp teeth show that it is a hunter.

Changing direction
The dorsal and ventral fins keep the fish from rolling when swimming.

A backbone without any bones!

Shark spinal column

Round discs of cartilage

Graceful swimmers
Sharks swim by beating their tails from side to side.

A rubbery backbone
A shark's skeleton is not made of bone at all. It is made of a hard, rubbery gristle called cartilage.

Skeleton suits

Most animals don't have a bony skeleton inside their bodies. Instead, insects, spiders, and most small sea creatures have a hard outer casing which supports and protects the soft body inside.

All around armor-plating

Turtle

Turtle skeleton

Skull

Vertebrae fused to shell

Neck bones

Webbed feet for swimming

Leg bones

Houselike shell
The turtle's skeleton is joined to its shell. The rigid rib bones cannot bend, so the turtle moves its head and limbs to pump air into its lungs.

Giant claws are for feeding and defense.

Armored beetle
Like other insects, the beetle is protected by a shell-like casing. Its delicate wings are tucked under hard wing cases.

Spiny spider crab

Eight walking legs

Wood-boring beetle

ime for a change!
crab crawls out of its shell skeleton once gets too small. The crab's body expands iickly and a new shell hardens over it.

The shell has lots of joints.

Old bones

How do we know about dinosaurs and other animals that lived in the past? From finding bones and teeth that have been preserved as fossils in rocks.

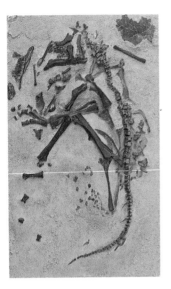

Fossil skeleton of young dinosaur

Dinosaur grave

When the remains of a dinosaur are found, the rock covering them has to be removed. The bones are then very carefully dug out.

Tail spikes for defense against hungry meat eaters

A deadly weapon

Piecing the clues together

Once dinosaur bones have been removed from rock, scientists try to fit them together. Missing bones are made from plaster.

Story in a skull
This fossil skull, with its massive jaws and serrated teeth, belonged to a fierce, meat-eating dinosaur.

Albertosaurus skull

Rebuilding the past

Reconstructed
Stegosaurus skeleton

Short front legs

Looking into the past
A large body, stumpy legs, and tiny head show us that this dinosaur was a slow-moving plant eater. The Stegosaurus lived more than 100 million years ago!

Broad, flat feet like an elephant's

Index

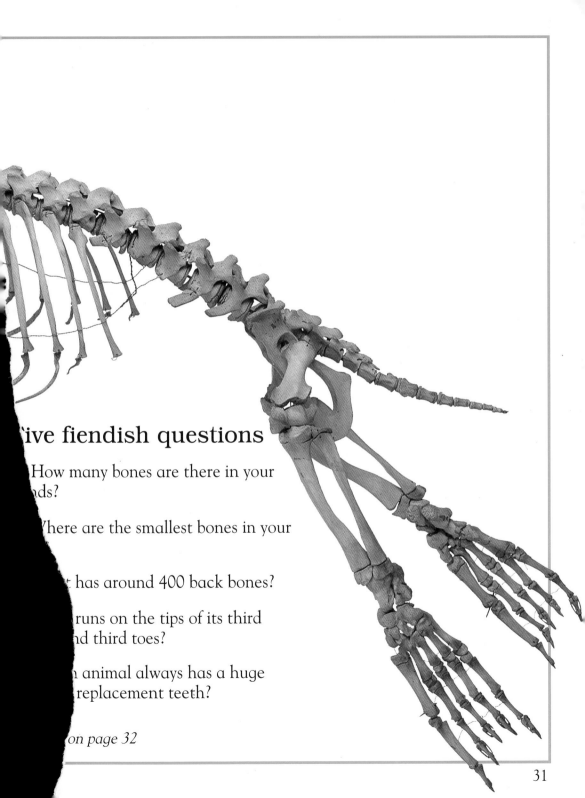

ive fiendish questions

How many bones are there in your
ds?

here are the smallest bones in your

has around 400 back bones?

runs on the tips of its third
d third toes?

animal always has a huge
replacement teeth?

on page 32

Answers

From page 31:

1. 27
2. Inside your ears
3. A snake
4. A horse
5. A shark

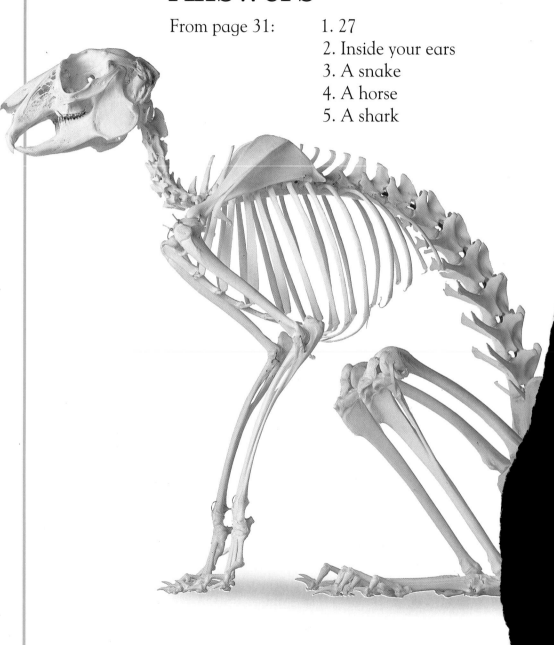